SPOTLIGHT ON SOCIAL AND EMOTIONAL LEARNING

A CAN-DO ATTITUDE

UNDERSTANDING SELF-EFFICACY

CAITIE MCANENEY

PowerKiDS press™

NEW YORK

Published in 2020 by The Rosen Publishing Group, Inc.
29 East 21st Street, New York, NY 10010

Copyright © 2020 by The Rosen Publishing Group, Inc.

Editor: Elizabeth Krajnik
Designer: Michael Flynn

Photo Credits: Cover Marc Romanelli/Blend Images/Getty Images; cover, pp. 1, 3–4, 6, 8, 10–12, 14–16, 18–20, 22–24 (background) TairA/Shutterstock.com; p. 5 Kyodo News/Getty Images; p. 6 Anson0618/Shutterstock.com; p. 7 Elena Elisseeva/Shutterstock.com; p. 9 JGI/Jamie Grill/Blend Images/Getty Images; p. 10 Africa Studio/Shutterstock.com; p. 11 VGstockstudio/Shutterstock.com; p. 13 Dmytro Vietrov/Shutterstock.com; p. 14 https://en.wikipedia.org/wiki/File:VanGogh-starry_night_ballance1.jpg; p. 15 Solis Images/Shutterstock.com; p. 17 Central Press/Hulton Archive/Getty Images; p. 18 My Life Graphic/Shutterstock.com; p. 19 Lucky Business/Shutterstock.com; p. 21 Patrick Smith/Getty Images Sport/Getty Images; p. 22 pathdoc/Shutterstock.com.

Cataloging-in-Publication Data

Names: McAneney, Caitie.
Title: A can-do attitude: understanding self-efficacy / Caitie McAneney.
Description: New York : PowerKids Press, 2020. | Series: Spotlight on social and emotional learning | Includes glossary and index.
Identifiers: ISBN 9781725301931 (pbk.) | ISBN 9781725301962 (library bound) | ISBN 9781725301948 (6pack)
Subjects: LCSH: Self-efficacy--Juvenile literature. | Self-esteem--Juvenile literature. | Goal (Psychology)--Juvenile literature.
Classification: LCC BF637.S38 M39 2020 | DDC 158.1--dc23

Manufactured in the United States of America

CPSIA Compliance Information: Batch #CSPK19. For further information contact Rosen Publishing, New York, New York at 1-800-237-9932.

CONTENTS

CHAPTER ONE

BELIEVE IN YOURSELF!

Have you ever wanted to do something really **difficult**? Maybe you wanted to learn how to do a cartwheel or solve a hard math problem or beat the next level on a video game. All of these things take practice and hard work. However, they also take a belief in your own ability. That's called self-efficacy.

Self-efficacy is the belief that you have the ability to succeed at a task or **achieve** a goal. When you believe in yourself, you're more likely to approach challenges in a different way than someone who doesn't believe in their abilities. You might work harder, overcome challenges, and be an active participant in the activity. Self-efficacy is all about control and **confidence**. You believe that you can control your actions and **attitude**. You have confidence that you can do anything you set your mind to. If you believe in yourself, you can't lose!

Simone Biles won four gold medals in women's artistic gymnastics at the 2016 Summer Olympics in Rio de Janeiro, Brazil. Without self-efficacy, Biles might not have trained so hard or had the confidence to fly through the air and stick the landing.

CHAPTER TWO

WHAT'S YOUR GOAL?

If you're good at something, it's easy to have self-efficacy. A gymnast who has trained for years will believe they can land a cartwheel with no problem. A chef will believe they can cook a great meal. However, this belief has come with years of hard work and **persistence**.

No one is good at everything. And no one is great at anything on the first try. That means many activities are challenges to overcome. The first step in achieving a certain outcome is **defining** your goal.

What goal do you want to achieve? It can be a goal for your schoolwork. For example, you might want to get a good grade on your science project. It can be a social goal, such as joining a new club or community center. It can relate to an **extracurricular** activity, such as scoring a goal in soccer.

Setting a goal is like defining a problem. That's the first step in problem solving!

SELF-AWARENESS

Having self-efficacy is just one part of being self-aware. To be aware is to have knowledge of something. To be self-aware is to have knowledge of yourself.

Have you ever seen the movie *Inside Out*? That movie shows how each person is made up of many **complex** emotions. You are also made up of your thoughts—including your opinions and judgments—and your values, or the things that are important to you.

You are a one-of-a-kind human being! And you have the ability to be an **expert** on yourself by being self-aware. This skill helps you define your emotions, thoughts, and values and **assess** your strengths and abilities. This helps you recognize your mindset when faced with a challenge. It can also tell you where you are in the process of achieving your goal and how you can achieve it in time.

Self-awareness skills include defining emotions, having self-confidence, and knowing your strengths.

CHAPTER FOUR

UNDERSTAND YOUR STRENGTHS

Knowing your strengths is one part of self-awareness. Some students are better at writing than they are at math. However, other students may be better at math than they are at writing. When we know our strengths, we can use them to achieve our goals.

First, write down a list of your strengths. What are you good at? What comes easily to you? What have you already worked on? You might be good at playing a sport, such as soccer or basketball. You might have a social strength, such as being a good listener or being respectful of others.

You must also know your limitations, or what you can't do. If you don't know how to program a robot, then you know you'll need to work extra hard to get better at coding.

How do you know what your strengths are? Think about the things people have praised you for in the past or the outcome of a past challenge. If you got an "A" on a computer programming assignment, coding might be one of your strengths.

CHAPTER FIVE

THE RIGHT ATTITUDE

Self-efficacy is all about approaching a challenge with the right attitude. If you think you can do something, then you'll work toward your goal with confidence. Self-confidence is the belief that you will succeed. People who are confident in their abilities are excited to work toward a goal. That attitude leads to motivation.

Motivation means that you have a desire, or want, to do something. If you have motivation, then you're driven toward accomplishing a task or reaching a goal. But what if you don't have motivation to work toward something? Imagine you're trying to learn piano, but you don't want to practice. Think about why you want to learn to play piano. Make a list of small goals you can achieve on your way to being a great pianist. Stay positive about practicing and remember: if you have the right attitude, you can do anything!

> To stay motivated, keep your eye on your goal and push through the setbacks and challenges that might come your way!

CHAPTER SIX

WHAT'S IN YOUR TOOLBOX?

Now you know your strengths and limitations. You have a can-do attitude and motivation. What else do you have? Before starting any big task, it's important to see what's in your toolbox. What do you have to work with?

Some of the best things in your toolbox are your experiences. What have you already done that can help you reach your goal? What have you learned that can help you accomplish a task?

The Starry Night is one of the most famous paintings of all time. Vincent van Gogh, a Dutch painter, used his past experiences with painting to create this masterpiece.

Make a list of experiences that have to do with the task at hand. Imagine you want to paint a picture of an elephant for an art competition. You've never done this before, and it seems like a big task. You then remember the times when you've mixed paint colors, drawn other animals, and watched elephants at the zoo. You have plenty of experiences that will help you reach your goal!

CHAPTER SEVEN

PICTURE THIS!

Another tool in your toolbox is your imagination. If you can picture yourself succeeding, then you will be more confident in your ability to reach your goal. This use of your imagination increases your belief in your own abilities. That will make you more likely to use the behaviors, such as practicing, that will get you closer to your goal.

This skill is also called visualization. Try it out! Imagine that you're going to run a race. The race is longer than you've ever run before. However, you have months to train before the race happens. Close your eyes and think about what it would look and feel like to finish that race. What would you see? What would you hear? What emotions would you feel? This picture of success can help you keep going even when your legs are tired and you want to give up.

Billie Jean King is a world-famous tennis star who won many titles in the 1960s and 1970s. She used visualization before tennis matches. She would imagine what could go wrong and how she would overcome **obstacles**.

CHAPTER EIGHT

WATCH AND LEARN

So far, you've used the tools of past experience and imagined experience. What else is in your toolbox? What other experiences can you use? You can use the experience of others!

Think of a teacher or **mentor** in your life who taught you a skill. Maybe your swim coach taught you how to swim the backstroke. That coach used knowledge they gained from their own experiences and passed it to you.

Reach out to others who have achieved a goal similar to yours. Send a letter or email to your favorite scientist, football player, or musician. They might write back with knowledge that can help you succeed!

You can learn a lot from other people just from observing, or watching, what they do. Watch a ballerina twirl around on a stage. Watch a family member cook dinner. Watch a snowboarder make their way down a hill. How do they accomplish the task? What does success look like? After you observe, ask questions! There's a lot to learn from others. And just remember, even an expert started out as a beginner.

CHAPTER NINE

BE PERSISTENT

Things worth achieving are rarely easy. That means you're going to face challenges along your path to success. However, the most important thing you can do in these moments is never give up.

One of the biggest roadblocks to success is the idea that your strengths and limitations are fixed, or unable to change. In this mindset, you're likely to say, "I'm just not good at science." However, you are always changing and learning and growing. With time, you can become strong at something or overcome a challenge. This is called a growth mindset. In this mindset, you might say, "I'm just not good at science . . . yet."

Being persistent, or not giving up, is one of the best tools for success. It means that you understand there will be challenges and that you might fail more than once, but you're willing to keep trying.

People who fall and get back up again are **resilient**. If you're resilient, you can get through anything in life.

CHAPTER TEN

MAKE A GAME PLAN!

You have all the tools you need and the right mindset. Can you achieve your goal? Yes, you can!

Where do you start? In any problem-solving situation, it's smart to make a game plan. Your goal might be a big one, and that can make it scary. However, if you break down that big goal into smaller parts, you have a greater chance of succeeding. Plus, you can celebrate all the smaller victories on the way to achieving your big goal. You don't have to run a great distance right away. Just run around the block!

Self-efficacy is like a superpower that you already have. All you have to do is believe in yourself. Identify your emotions and strengths, grow your self-confidence, and use every experience you can to achieve your goal. With hard work, persistence, and the right mindset, you can do anything!

GLOSSARY

achieve (uh-CHEEV) To get by effort.

assess (uh-SEHS) To decide the importance, size, or value of something.

attitude (AA-tuh-tood) A feeling or way of thinking that affects a person's behavior.

complex (kahm-PLEKS) Having to do with something with many parts.

confidence (KAHN-fuh-dens) A feeling of trust or belief.

define (duh-FYNE) To determine the qualities or meaning of something.

difficult (DIH-fih-kuhlt) Hard to do, make, or carry out.

expert (EHK-spurt) Someone who knows a great deal about something.

extracurricular (ehk-struh-kuh-RIH-kyuh-luhr) Of or relating to activities that aren't a part of a course of study in school.

mentor (MEHN-tohr) Someone who provides advice and support to a less experienced person.

obstacle (AHB-stuh-kuhl) Something that stops forward movement or progress.

persistence (puhr-SIH-stuhnts) The act of persisting, or continuing to do something in spite of challenges.

resilient (ruh-ZIHL-yuhnt) Having the ability to recover from or adjust to misfortune or change.

INDEX

PRIMARY SOURCE LIST

Page 5
U.S. gymnast Simone Biles performs in the women's floor exercise final at the Rio de Janeiro Olympics on Aug. 16, 2016. Photograph. Kyodo News.

Page 14
The Starry Night. Oil on canvas. Vincent van Gogh. 1889. Now kept at the Museum of Modern Art, New York City.

Page 17
American tennis player Billie Jean Moffitt, later Billie Jean King, playing at Wimbledon. Photograph. Central Press. ca. 1965.

WEBSITES

Due to the changing nature of Internet links, PowerKids Press has developed an online list of websites related to the subject of this book. This site is updated regularly. Please use this link to access the list: www.powerkidslinks.com/SSEL/cando